Cor tion 1

Michael
Dean

Longman

Unit 1 The Youth Club

Writing about you and your family

Completing sentences

Tell your partner, then complete the sentences.

My father is ________________________ . (a teacher? a businessman?)

My mother is ________________________ . (a housewife? an engineer?)

My brother is ________________________ . (at school? a pilot?)

My sister is ________________________ . (at school? a nurse?)

1 **Complete the form and the sentences about Paul Reynolds. The sentences help you with the form and the form helps you with the sentences.**

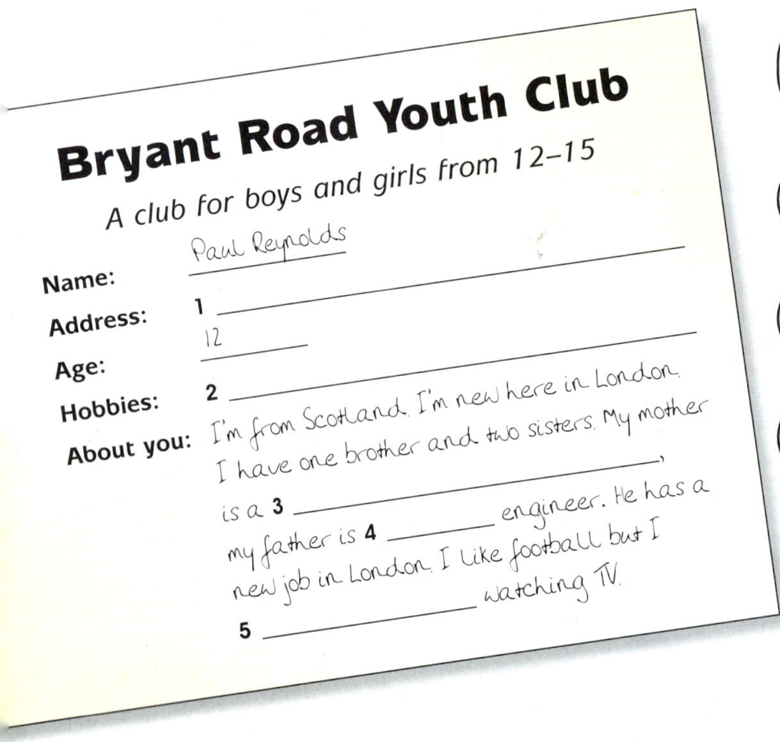
Bryant Road Youth Club

A club for boys and girls from 12–15

Name: Paul Reynolds

Address: 1 ________________

Age: 12

Hobbies: 2 ________________

About you: I'm from Scotland. I'm new here in London.
I have one brother and two sisters. My mother
________,
is a 3 ________
my father is 4 ________ engineer. He has a
new job in London. I like football but I
________ watching TV.
5 ________

2 **Complete the sentences.**

My hobbies are ____ .

I like ____ .

I don't like ____ .

Writing sentences

3 Work with a partner. Write the sentences (a–c) in the correct place in the dialogue. Then say the dialogue together.

a All my family like quizzes.

b I don't like table tennis.

c My brother Tom likes films, but I don't.

It's Paul's first time at Bryant Road Youth Club. He's with his new friend, Robert.

4 Write sentences.

Write five sentences about what you and your family like and don't like doing.
Example: My mother doesn't like watching TV.

Putting sentences together

5 Write the two sentences again as one sentence, using *but* or *so*.

Examples:

Paul likes football and table tennis. He doesn't like watching TV.

Paul likes football and table tennis but he doesn't like watching TV.

All my family like quizzes. We all go to the quiz at the club on Monday.

All my family like quizzes so we all go to the quiz at the club on Monday

1 Paul Reynolds doesn't like films. His brother Tom does.
2 Paul has one brother and two sisters. Robert has a big family.
3 Paul likes table tennis. He plays at the youth club on Thursday.
4 Robert's father is a businessman. Paul's father is an engineer.
5 Paul and Robert are friends now. They go to the youth club together.

6 Write a paragraph.

We want information about you and your family for the Voyager 3 spaceship. Write about you and your family for anybody in space who wants to know about life here.

Write about:

- your name, how old you are and where you live.
- your hobbies, what you do in your free time and what you don't like doing.
- how many brothers and sisters you have.
- what your brothers and sisters do in their free time.
- your mother's and father's jobs and what they do in their free time.

Unit 2 The wrong room

Writing about your day at school

Completing sentences

What time do you start and finish school? Which subjects have you got today?

1 Complete the timetable and the sentences. The timetable helps you with the sentences and the sentences help you with the timetable.

TIMETABLE: ROBERT SIMPSON, CLASS 7. *All lessons are in room 25*

	9.00–9.50	9.50–10.10	10.40–11.30	11.30–12.20	1.30–2.20	2.30–3.10
Monday	art (art room)	French	maths	religious education	history	PSE*
Tuesday	science (science room)	1 ______	technology	German	PE** (gym)	PE
Wednesday	English	maths	science (science room)	technology	French	geography
Thursday	English	German	technology	music (music room)	2 ______	history
Friday	science (science room)	English	English	maths	music (music room)	religious education

* Personal and Social Education. It's about you and your world. ** Physical Education

We have geography before technology on Tuesday. Maths is after music on Thursday. Religious education is **3** ______ maths on Monday. English is **4** ______ German on Thursday.

The lesson from 1.30 to 2.20 on Monday is **5** ______. The lesson from **6** ______ to **7** ______ on Tuesday is technology. The first technology lesson of the week is **8** ______ 10.40 **9** ______ 11.30 on Tuesday.

2 Complete the sentences.

How is your timetable different from Robert's?
What do you like about your timetable and Robert's?

We have ______, but Robert has ______ .

On ______ we ______ but Robert ______ .

We have ______ and I like that but Robert has ______ and that's nice.

Writing sentences

3 Work with a partner. Write the sentences (a–c) in the correct place in the dialogue. Then say the dialogue together.

a 9.00–9.50 on Monday we have history, not art.

b But most of our lessons are in room 25.

c After art we have French.

It's the first day of the new year at school. Paul and Robert are outside the art room.

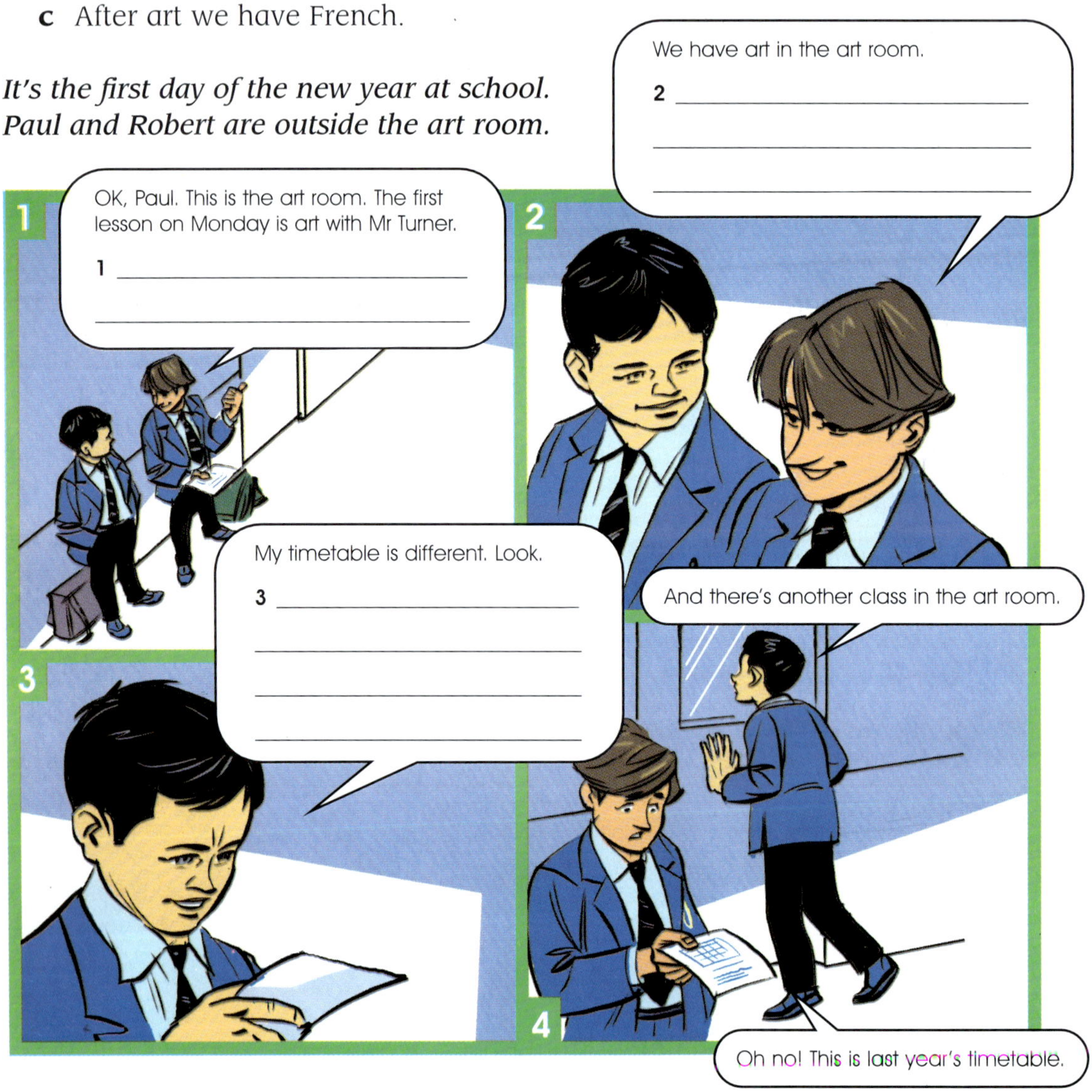

4 Write sentences.

Write your timetable and then write five sentences about it.
Examples:

On Monday from 11.20 to 12.10 I have English with Mr Smith.

Most of our lessons are in room 25 but we have art in the art room.

Putting sentences together

5 Look at Robert's timetable again. Write sentences like the example.

Example:

Monday: French – maths (after)

On Monday Robert has maths after French

1 Thursday – science – English (before)
2 Wednesday – English and maths – science (after)
3 Tuesday – PE – in the gym – German (after)
4 Friday – music – maths (after)
5 Tuesday – science – geography (before)

6 Write a paragraph.

Work with a partner. Write a dream timetable. Then write a paragraph of five or six sentences about your dream timetable and why you like it.

Write about:

- the subjects on the dream timetable.
- when school starts and finishes on your dream timetable.
- which days you have school.
- what you like about your dream timetable.

Writing Tip

Capital letters: **E**nglish, **M**onday, **P**aul but not **g**eography

Unit 3 I have some nice friends.

Writing descriptions of people

Completing sentences

Write more words about your friends:

height: tall, ______________________

colour of hair: brown, ______________________

likes: ______________________

1 Use the words on the photos to complete the letter and use the letter to complete the words on the photos.

This is the one who is **1** ________ ________ ________. He's a tall boy and very funny

This is the **2** ________ who helps me with maths.

This is the one who lives near me. He has long **3** ________ hair. I go to the club with him

Dear Joe,

Here are photos of three of my new friends at the club, where I go every week now.

The one with the brown hair is Robert. He's the one who I go to the **4** ________ with. He's very nice and very clever but he thinks other people are stupid! He always tells me things I know.

Simon always makes jokes. He always makes everybody laugh. He's very **5** ________ and very thin. He's fantastic at art.

Melanie is the one **6** ________ helps me with my maths homework sometimes. She's very clever. She's the one with the red hair, in the photo.

2 Complete the sentences.

Write about your friends.

My friend ________ has ________________________.

My friend ________ is ________________________.

My friend ________ likes ________________________.

Writing sentences

3 Work with a partner. Write the sentences (a–c) in the correct place in the dialogue. Then say the dialogue together.

a He's always very happy.
b He's a very helpful person.
c She's the one with the red hair.

Paul is talking on the telephone with his friend Joe.

4 Write sentences.

Write six sentences about your friends.
example: My friend Tom is very thin.
example: My friend Jane is very clever.
example: My friend John is fantastic at football.

Putting sentences together

5 Write the two sentences again as one sentence, using *who* or *where*.

Examples:

This is the club. I go to the club every week now.

This is the club, where I go every week now.

This is Robert. Robert lives near me.

This is Robert, who lives near me.

1 This is Robert. Robert is the one with brown hair in the photo.

2 Paul goes to the club with Robert. Robert is his best friend.

3 Paul likes Simon. Simon is fantastic at art and is unusual.

4 Paul sees all his friends at the club. He plays table tennis at the club.

5 After German we go to the gym. We have PE in the gym.

7 Write a paragraph.

You are sending a group photo of your friends to a pen friend.
Write about one of your friends, who is in the photo.

Write about:

- what your friend looks like.
- what sort of person your friend is.
- what your friend is good at.

Writing Tip

He **is** good at football. She **has** black hair.

Unit 4 A letter to a pen friend

Writing an informal letter

Completing sentences

Write a sentence about yourself to a pen friend.
Read the sentence to your partner.

---

1 Use the words on the drawings to complete the letter and use the letter to complete the words on the drawings.

When I leave school
I want to be a
4 ______________
______________.

Simon's World

This is our house.
It's a **1** __________ British house.
My bedroom is at the **2** __________
on the left.

A **3** __________ with friends.
This is me, Paul and Robert.

Dear Greg,
Here are three drawings of **5** '__________ World'.
I like drawing. Art is my favourite subject at
school. One day I **6** ________ ________ ________ a
commercial artist and do the drawings in books.
My mum and dad are doctors. We live in a
typical **7** __________ house. My bedroom is at
the top, on the **8** __________ in the drawing.
It's a small room. Sometimes, in the summer,
my friends and I have a picnic. In the drawing
you can see me, Paul **9** __________ Robert.
Tell me about your life in New York.
Best wishes,
Simon

2 Complete the sentences.

When I leave school I ______________________________.

We live ______________________________.

Sometimes I ______________________________.

Writing sentences

3 Work with a partner. Write the sentences (a–c) in the correct place in the dialogue. Then say the dialogue together.

a He also lives in Queens.
b One day I want to open a store too.
c We play baseball together too.

Simon and his pen friend Greg, from New York, are chatting on the Internet. Simon is interviewing Greg for the school newspaper.

4 Write sentences.

Write five sentences to a pen friend. Tell your pen friend about your world.
examples:

I live near my school.
My big brother is an engineer.

Putting sentences together

5 Write the sentences again using *and*, *also* and *too*.

Examples:

Simon has a small room. His sister has a small room.

a Simon and his sister have small rooms.

b Simon has a small room. His sister has a small room too.

c Simon has a small room. His sister also has a small room.

Be careful!

Simon's dad is a doctor. Simon's mum is a doctor.
Simon's dad is a doctor. His mum *is also* (not *also is*) a doctor.

1 Paul likes table tennis. His brother Tom likes table tennis.

2 Simon lives in Rutland Street. Paul lives in Rutland Street.

3 Paul is good at English. Melanie is good at English.

6 Write a letter.

Write to your pen friend in England or America. Tell your pen friend about:

- where you live.
- who your friends are.
- what you do with your friends.
- your family – your mum and dad, your brothers and sisters. What do they do?

Writing Tip

Start: **Dear ________ ,**
Finish: **Best wishes,**

Unit 5 An e-mail about food

Writing about what you like to eat

Completing sentences

List food that you like and food that you don't like. Read your lists to a partner.

I like ____ .

I don't like ____ .

1 Use the questionnaire to complete the e-mail and the e-mail to complete the questionnaire.

Questionnaire

Class 8 Trip to Surrey Study Centre. Please fill in this questionnaire about the food you like and don't like.

Name: Laura Hanson

breakfast:	*like*	*don't like*
cereal	✓	☐
1 ________	✓	☐
toast	✓	☐
butter	✓	☐
eggs	✓	☐
baked beans	✓	☐
drinks:		
tea	✓	☐
2 ________	☐	✓

lunch and dinner:	*like*	*don't like*
meat:		
– lamb	✓	☐
– **3** ________	✓	☐
– beef	☐	✓
fish	✓	☐
salad	✓	☐
vegetables:		
– tomatoes	☐	✓
– peas	✓	☐
– potatoes	✓	☐
drinks:		
– cola	☐	✓
– **4** ________	✓	☐

On weekdays I have a quick breakfast. I usually have **5** ________ (like cornflakes) with milk and a cup of **6** ________. I never drink coffee. On Saturday we have a full English breakfast with toast and butter, eggs and baked beans because we have more time at the weekend.

For lunch I have chicken, lamb or sometimes fish because I want something hot, although I never have **7** ________. I don't eat it. I usually have a salad with my lunch and a glass of lemonade.

We have dinner at 7.30. We sometimes have lamb and sometimes chicken with potatoes and **11** ________.

2 Complete the sentences.

What do you eat for breakfast, lunch and dinner?

For breakfast I usually have ____________ but sometimes I have ____________ .

For lunch I usually ____________________ but sometimes ____________________ .

For dinner I usually ____________________ but ____________________________ .

Writing sentences

3 Work with a partner. Write the sentences (a–c) in the correct place in the dialogue. Then say the dialogue together.

a I usually have cornflakes because I like a small breakfast.

b We never have beef.

c I eat most things although I prefer something hot.

Next week, in the school holidays, Laura is staying with her friend Jane in the north of England. Laura and Jane are talking about food.

4 Write sentences.

Write five sentences about what you and your family eat: Use *sometimes*, *usually*, *always* or *never* in each sentence.

Putting sentences together

5 Write the two sentences again as one sentence, using *because* or *although*.

Examples:

I don't have sandwiches for lunch. I like something hot.

I don't have sandwiches for lunch because I like something hot.

I usually have a small breakfast. I have a big breakfast on Saturday.

I usually have a small breakfast although I have a big breakfast on Saturday.

1. I don't like meat very much. I eat lamb sometimes.
2. I don't usually have a big breakfast. There is no time before school starts.
3. I like vegetables and salad. Most of my friends don't.
4. I have a cup of tea after school. I always want something to drink before I start my homework.
5. I have a cup of tea after school. I don't have any biscuits or cakes.

6 Write a paragraph.

Write to a friend about what you and your family usually eat and drink. Tell your friend what you and your family:

- usually have for breakfast.
- usually have for lunch and dinner.
- eat and drink at other times.
- don't eat and drink.

Then write more about the food and drink of the country where you live.

Writing Tip

We always/usually/sometimes/never have ...

Unit 6 It's party time!

Writing party invitations

Completing sentences

What do you eat and drink at a party? Talk with a partner, then write.

____

1 Look at the note, the invitation and the map and complete the sentences.

April 7

Paul,

We can have your welcome party at my house **1** ________ 1.30 **2** ________ 6 PM **3** ________ Friday 20.
We can ask Simon to draw a **4** ________ of Rutland Street with the **5** ________ five and number **6** ________ bus routes on it, or I can draw it myself.

All the best,
Robert

Invitation

Please come to Paul's **7** ________ *party* **8** ________ *my house. The party is from* **1.30** *PM to* **6** *PM on* **9** ________ .
Robert Simpson

Please complete the reply slip below:

I can/cannot come to Paul's welcome party
Name: ____________

2 Complete the sentences.

Talk about your dream party with a partner and write what you both want.
Who do you want at your dream party? You can have anybody you like.

I would like ______________________________ at my party.

Where do you want your dream party?

I want my party ______________________________

What do you want to do at your dream party? Talk? Eat? Watch films?

I want to ______________________________ at my dream party.

Writing sentences

3 Work with a partner. Write the sentences (a–c) in the correct places in the dialogue. Then say the dialogue together.

a They can get a number five or a number eleven.

b They can get off at the police station or Rutland Street.

c Inside is OK, although a barbecue outside is better.

Robert and Paul are talking at Robert's house.

4 Write sentences.

You are having a party at your house.

1. When is the party? (time, day and date)
2. How can guests get to your party?
3. What sort of party are you having? (Barbecue? Picnic? Films?)
4. Write a reply slip for your party invitation.

Putting sentences together

5 Write these sentences again with *or* or *although*.

Example: You can get a number five bus. You can get a number eleven bus.

You can get a number five or you can get a number eleven bus.

We can have the party indoors. A party outside is better.

We can have the party indoors although a party outside is better.

1 Robert can draw the map. Simon can draw the map.

2 Robert can draw the map. Simon can draw the map better.

3 You can get off at the police station. The Rutland Street bus stop is quicker.

4 Some people only like to talk at parties. Most people like to talk and eat something.

5 We can have a reply slip on the invitation. People can telephone you if they are coming.

6 Write a note, an invitation and a map with information on it.

Work with a partner. Write a note asking a friend if he wants a party, write a party invitation with a reply slip and draw a map. On the map, write how to get to the party.

Writing Tip

Don't forget to put the date at the top of your note.

Unit 7 Where is everything?

Writing about your room

Completing sentences

What have you got in your bedroom at home? Read your answer to a partner.

____

1 **Use the words on the picture to complete the sentences and use the sentences to complete the words on the picture.**

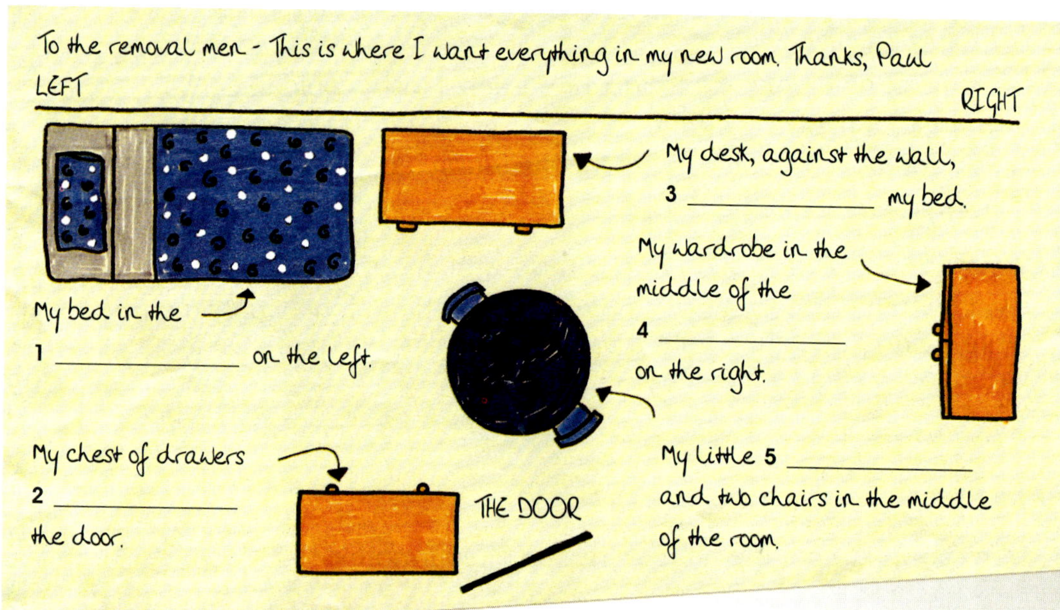

Please put the following things against the wall:
my bed in the corner on the **6** ______________ and my **7** ______________ near my bed. Please
put the little table and two **8** ______________ in the **9** ______________ of **10** ______________ room.
I want my **11** ______________ in the middle of the wall on the **12** ______________ please. And one more
thing - please put my **13** ______________ ______ ______________ by the door. Thank you!
Paul

2 **Complete the sentences about you.**

I've got a ______________ and a ______________ in my room.

My ______________ is ______________ .

I have ______________ too. They are ______________ .

Writing sentences

3 Work with a partner. Write the sentences (a–c) in the correct places in the dialogue. Then say the dialogue together.

a I'm at my desk in my new room.

b The chairs are by the window.

c 'Please put the little table and two chairs in the middle of the room.'

Paul is in his bedroom on the first day in his new home in London. He is on the phone to his friend Joe in Scotland.

4 Write sentences.

Draw a plan of your room for the removal men. Write five sentences to the removal men. Tell them where you want everything.

Examples: Please put the wardrobe against the wall on the right.
I want the table and chairs in the middle of the room, please.

Putting sentences together

5 Write the two sentences again as one sentence, using *These are the things I want ... :* or *Please put the following things ... :*

Examples:

I want the bed near the door, please. I want the tables and chairs near the door, please.

These are the things I want near the door, please: the bed, the table and chairs.

Please put the bed near the door. Please put the tables and chairs near the door.

Please put the following things near the door: the bed, the table and chairs.

1. I want the computer on my desk, please. I want my school books, my pencils, my pens and my CD player on my desk please.
2. Please put my wardrobe by the door. Please put my chest of drawers and my bed by the door.
3. I want my bed in the corner on the right, please. I want my little table and my books in the corner on the right, please.
4. Please put my mirror on the wall. Please put my posters and my drawings on the wall.
5. I want my clothes in the wardrobe, please. I want my small mirror, my old books and my photos in the wardrobe please.

6 Write a paragraph.

Write a note to the removal men. Tell them where to put everything in your room. Then write another note to the removal men. Tell them where to put everything in another room of your house or flat.

Writing Tip

Please **put** ... Please **don't put** ...

Composition 1: teacher's notes and answer key

The characters

Composition 1 has a cast of characters living in London who are the same age as your pupils. As as well doing everyday things like having fun at youth clubs and not so everyday things like going to the Moon, the characters do some of the same tasks that your pupils do. For example, they write stories and then the pupils write them. So these characters are a point of interest for pupils as well as realistic language models for writing.

The structure of the book

All the units in Composition 1 have this structure:
Page 1 – Completing sentences
Page 2 – Writing sentences
Page 3 – Putting sentences together

The structure of each unit

Page 1 – Completing sentences

What the pupils write on page 1 is used again on pages 2 and 3.

Warm up
The first task gets the pupils thinking about the subject of the unit and it starts them writing single words or lists. Pupils often tell their partner what they have written, so learning to write is supported by using English orally.

Task 1
In task 1 pupils are shown two different pieces of communication. In unit 1 these are an application form and somebody speaking. Both pieces of communication are gapped and the gaps from one can be written in by reading and understanding the other piece of communication.

Task 2: Complete the sentences.
In task 2 pupils complete sentences about themselves and their world, within the theme of the unit. In unit 1 they write about their own hobbies and activities, having learned about the hobbies of an English boy of their own age in task 1.

Page 2 – Writing sentences

What pupils write on page 2 is used again on page 3.

Task 3
In task 3 pupils work in pairs and write three given sentences in the correct places in a cartoon dialogue. They then say the dialogue together. The three sentences continue the themes introduced on page 1 and introduce the linking task, task 5, on page 3. As with the warm-up task, oral work is used to help the acquisition of writing skills and to make learning fun. In unit 4 the cartoon is about two boys at a youth club, talking about what they and their family like and don't like doing.

Task 4: Write sentences
This is the sentence-level free stage. From here until the end of the unit, pupils write in their exercise books, not in the textbook. Pupils write five sentences of their own about the theme of the unit. In unit 1 the sentences are about what the pupil and the family like and don't like doing, so weaker pupils can draw directly on the sentences they completed in task 3 but they also have to take another step in their writing skills and write about the family, helped by task 4.

Page 3 – Putting sentences together

Task 5
Task 5 helps pupils to join two sentences in two different ways. The ways of joining sentences have been introduced earlier in the unit and so has all the vocabulary in this task.

Task 6: Write a paragraph
Task 6 is the culmination of the unit. Pupils write a paragraph, or an invitation or a note depending on the theme of the unit. Guidance is given that refers pupils back to their earlier work in the unit, but in some units they are also invited to write a little more, unguided.

Answer key

UNIT 1

1 1 185 Rutland Street, London 2 football, table tennis and quizzes 3 housewife 4 an 5 don't like 6 12 7 one 8 sisters

3 1b 2c 3a

5 1 Paul Reynolds doesn't like films but his brother Tom does.
2 Paul has one brother and two sisters but Robert has a big family.
3 Paul likes table tennis so he plays at the youth club on Thursday.
4 Robert's father is a businessman but Paul's father is an engineer.
5 Paul and Robert are friends now so they go to the youth club together.

UNIT 2

1 1 geography 2 maths 3 after 4 before 5 history 6 10.40 7 11.30 8 from 9 to

3 1c 2b 3a

5 1 On Thursday, Robert has science before English.
2 On Wednesday, Robert has science after English and maths.
3 On Tuesday, Robert has PE in the gym after German.
4 On Friday, Robert has music after maths.
5 On Tuesday, Robert has science before geography.

UNIT 3

1 1 fantastic at art 2 one 3 brown 4 club 5 tall 6 who

3 1b 2c 3a

5 1 This is Robert, who has brown hair in the photo.
2 Paul goes to the club with Robert, who is his best friend.
3 Paul likes Simon, who is fantastic at art and is unusual.
4 Paul sees all his friends at the club, where he plays table tennis.
5 After German, we go to the gym, where we have PE.

UNIT 4

1 1 typical 2 top 3 picnic 4 commercial artist 5 Simon's 6 want to be 7 British 8 left 9 and

3 1c 2a 3b

5 1 **a** Paul and his brother Tom like table tennis.
b Paul likes table tennis. His brother Tom likes table tennis too.
c Paul likes table tennis. His brother Tom also likes table tennis.

2 **a** Simon and Paul live in Rutland Street.
b Simon lives in Rutland Street. Paul lives in Rutland Street too.
c Simon lives in Rutland Street. Paul also lives in Rutland Street.

3 **a** Paul and Melanie are good at English.
b Paul is good at English. Melanie is good at English too.
c Paul is good at English. Melanie is also good at English.

UNIT 5

1 1 milk 2 coffee 3 chicken 4 lemonade 5 cereal 6 tea 7 beef 8 peas

3 1a 2c 3b

5 1 I don't like meat very much although I eat lamb sometimes.
2 I don't usually have a big breakfast because there is no time before school starts.
3 I like vegetables and salad although most of my friends don't.
4 I have a cup of tea after school because I always want something to drink before I start my homework.
5 I have a cup of tea after school although I don't have any biscuits or cakes.

UNIT 6

1 1 from 2 to 3 on 4 map 5 number
6 eleven 7 welcome 8 at
9 Friday 20 April

3 1c 2a 3b

5 1 Robert can draw the map or Simon can draw it.
2 Robert can draw the map although Simon can draw it better.
3 You can get off at the police station although the Rutland Street bus stop is quicker.
4 Some people only like to talk at parties although most people like to talk and eat something.
5 We can have a reply slip on the invitation or people can telephone you if they are coming.

UNIT 7

1 1 corner 2 by 3 near 4 wall 5 table
6 left 7 desk 8 chairs 9 middle 10 the
11 wardrobe 12 right 13 chest of drawers

3 1a 2c 3b

5 1 These are the things I want on my desk please: my school books, pencils, pens and CD player.
2 Please put the following things by the door: my wardrobe, chest of drawers and bed.
3 These are the things I want in the corner on the right, please: my bed, little table and books.
4 Please put the following things on the wall: my mirror, posters and drawings.
5 These are the things I want in the wardrobe: my small mirror, old books and photo.

UNIT 8

Warm up: access, provider, screen, click, mouse, e-mail

1 1 screen 2 printer 3 power 4 mouse
5 e-mail 6 'File'

3 1b 2a 3c

5 1 First you press the power button, secondly you wait for the computer to be ready.
2 You move the mouse on the mouse mat and then you see the arrow on the screen.
3 You click the mouse and after that access the provider.
4 You get the message on the screen and then you print it.
5 You do all these things to download your e-mails and lastly you read them.

UNIT 9

1 1 adventure 2 cabin 3 woods 4 driving
5 in 6 watching 7 centre 8 barbecue
9 teenagers 10 entertainment 11 last

3 1c 2a 3b

5 1 We aren't writing to Paul and Robert. We are seeing them tomorrow.
2 I've got a stamp. It's in my wallet.
3 You can do anything at the entertainment centre. It has rooms where you can sit and read or write postcards.
4 Look, there are Melanie and Peter. They're driving go-karts.
5 That's a number five bus. It stops near Robert's house.

UNIT 10

1 1 first 2 Happy 3 fan club
4 membership 5 send 6 T-shirt 7 year

3 1b 2a 3c

5 Dear Peter Hurst,
I watch a lot of English football and I think Liverpool are the best team in the world. Please send me an autographed photo of you in a number nine shirt.

Dear Delores Smith,
I think you are a really great actress and I want to join your fan club. I have a question for you: Who is your favourite actor?

UNIT 11

1 1 Main 2 pool 3 supermarket 4 butcher's 5 food 6 store 7 swimming 8 café

3 1c 2a 3b

5 1 There's a beautiful park in the centre of the city so people from the offices can go for a walk. **OR** People from the offices can go for a walk because there's a beautiful park in the centre of the city.
2 There's a bus stop near the cinema because a lot of people want to go home by bus after the film. **OR** There's a bus stop near the cinema so a lot of people want to go home by bus after the film.
3 There is a café near here so we can sit down.
4 There's a café near the shops so a lot of people like to have a cup of coffee after going shopping. **OR** There's a café near the shops because a lot of people like to have a cup of coffee after going shopping.
5 I want a helipad near my house because I don't want to walk to school every day.

UNIT 12

1 1 had 2 bicycle 3 swimming 4 ate 5 Friday 6 breakfast 7 sky 8 tables

3 1b 2a 3c

5 1 We went swimming. It was the best thing we did all week.
2 We played table tennis and football. I really enjoyed it.
3 We went shopping a lot. It was great.
4 I taught a friend to swim. It was difficult.
5 I helped my friend with his homework. I enjoyed it very much.

UNIT 13

1 1 thirsty 2 glass 3 pair 4 shoes 5 sleeve 6 lemonade 7 street 8 leg 9 trousers

2 1 The monster was looking for a man who was like a father to him.
2 The police had a red shirt with them when they came.
3 It was later that evening when the police came to the boy's house.

3 1c 2b 3a

5 1 I was walking home when I stopped for a drink of lemonade at a café.
2 The café is in a small dark street where nobody lives.
3 I was feeling unhappy when I saw my friend.
4 I felt bad when I ate all day.
5 This is the big house where the monster lives.

UNIT 14

1 1 Kill 2 monster 3 Excuse me 4 use 5 afraid 6 was looking for 7 the 8 mobile phone 9 who

3 1a 2b 3c

5 1 I knew a boy who told good stories.
2 There was a café near here which had three big rooms.
3 We were looking for the monster which had got our friend.
4 My friends found the place which was secret.
5 I wanted to use the mobile phone which the man had in his hand.

Unit 8 How do you get e-mail?

Writing instructions

Completing sentences

Work with a partner. Which of these words are about computers?

access, oil, provider, screen, car key, click, cat, mouse, e-mail, petrol

Can you write any more words about computers?

____

1 Use the diagrams to complete the instructions and the instructions to complete the diagrams.

Diagram 1

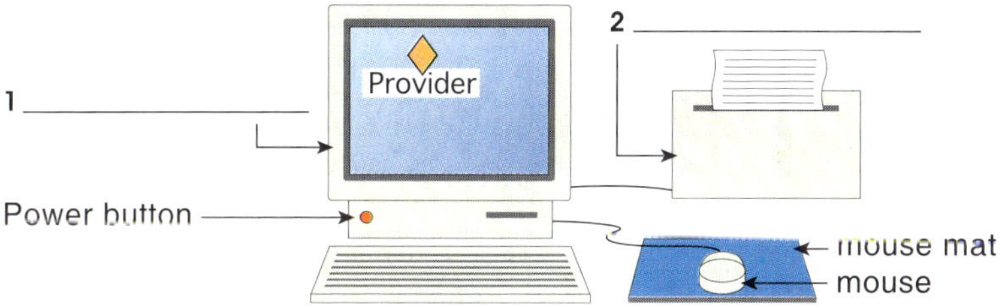

Diagram 2

Instructions

1 Press the **3** ______________ button under the screen. Don't touch the printer, on the right of the computer.

2 Move the **4** ______________ on the mouse mat until the arrow points to 'Provider'.

3 Click on 'Provider' with the mouse and you get a new screen (look at the second diagram).

4 On the new screen click on 'Get **5** ______________'.

5 When you see the e-mail message click on **6** ______________ in the little box.

2 Complete the sentences.

I like these machines: ______________________________

I don't like these machines: ______________________________

I like ______________ because ______________________________ .

I don't like ______________ because ______________________________ .

Writing sentences

3 Work with a partner. Write the sentences (a–c) in the correct place in the dialogue. Then say the dialogue together.

a The next thing is to access the provider.

b First, you switch it on.

c Don't forget to file the message.

Next week Laura is staying with Jane in the north of England. Before she goes, she is showing her father how to download her e-mails.

4 Write one sentence from instructions for four different machines.

Start each sentence with *Don't forget to* or *Remember to*. Then read your sentences to a partner. Your partner has to guess which machine each time.
Example: Don't forget to start the engine. (Answer: car)

Putting sentences together

5 Put the sentences together in the correct order.

Example:

You file it.
You look at the e-mail message. (and after that)

You look at the e-mail message and after that you file it.

1 You wait for the computer to be ready.
You press the power button. (first, secondly)

2 You move the mouse on the mouse mat.
You see the arrow on the screen. (and then)

3 You click the mouse.
You access the provider. (and after that)

4 You get the message on the screen.
You print it. (and then)

5 You read them.
You do all these things to download your e-mails. (and lastly)

6 Write instructions.

Work with a partner. Write instructions for doing something.
You can write instructions to use any machine, like a car or a mobile phone. You can write instructions to cook something (a recipe).

Writing Tip

First ..., secondly ..., thirdly ..., fourthly ..., lastly ...

Unit 9 A holiday postcard

Writing postcards

Completing sentences

Where do you want to go for a holiday? Compare your answers with a partner.

____

1 Use the postcard to complete the brochure and the brochure to complete the postcard.

Dear Laura,

I am on an **1** ____________ *holiday for teenagers. I'm staying in a* **2** ____________ *in the* **3** ____________ *with five other girls. My little brother Peter is staying in the boys' cabin. It's really nice here. Tomorrow we're* **4** ____________ *a go-kart* **5** ________ *the woods and the next day we're* **6** ____________ *a film in the entertainment* **7** ____________. *Great! There's a* **8** ____________ *on the last day too.*

Best wishes,

Melanie

Adventure Holidays for 9 ____________.

Stay in a cabin in the woods – better than a hotel!

Drive a go-kart in the woods.

Watch films in our modern 10 ____________ centre.

And on the 11 ________ day there's an unforgettable barbecue.

2 Complete the sentences.

Plan your dream holiday. You can be with anybody and do anything you want.

I am going to go to ____________________ with ____________________.

We are going to ____.

Writing sentences

3 Work with a partner. Write the sentences (a–c) in the correct place in the dialogue. Then say the dialogue together.

a There is a modern entertainment centre here, too.
b Yes, they're in my wallet.
c We're having a great time here.

Melanie and Peter are writing postcards in a room at the entertainment centre in the evening.

4 Write sentences.

Write five sentences saying what a good time you are having on holiday.
Example: Paris is really beautiful.

Putting sentences together

Write the two sentences again as one sentence, using *they're, them, it's* or *it*.

Example:

The postcards aren't on the table.
The postcards are over there.

The postcards aren't on the table. They're over there.

1 We aren't writing to Paul and Robert.
We are seeing Paul and Robert tomorrow.

2 I've got a stamp.
The stamp is in my wallet.

3 You can do anything at the entertainment centre.
The entertainment centre has rooms where you can sit and read or write postcards.

4 Look, there are Melanie and Peter.
Melanie and Peter are driving go-karts.

5 That's a number five bus.
The number five bus stops near Robert's house.

6 Write a postcard.

Write a postcard to Paul Reynolds. First write the greeting, the ending and Paul's address.

Then write a postcard to Paul. Tell him:

- where you are, on holiday.
- what you are doing.
- how nice it is.
- where you are going tomorrow and the next day.

Then write about your own idea.

Writing Tip

Paul Reynolds's address is in Unit 1.
The greeting and the ending for postcards are on the first page of this unit.

Unit 10 I am a fan of yours.

Writing letters requesting something

Completing sentences

Write the names of three stars you like (film stars, sports stars or pop stars). Has your partner got the same names?

____

1 Use the fan letter and the fan club information to complete the sentences.

Dear Delores Smith,
I am a big fan of yours.
I loved your **1** ________
film 'Me and My Cat' and
I really liked '**2** ________
in L.A.' too.
I would like to join the
3 ________ ________. I enclose
$20 for **4** ________
for one year.
Please also **5** ________ me
a photo and a Delores Smith
6 ________.
Best wishes,
Melanie Dexter

The Delores Smith Fan Club

membership $20 a **7** ________

About Delores Smith

Born:
January 22, 1980 in New York
First film:
'Me and My Cat' (1991)
Other films:
'Happy in L.A'. (1995)
'We Are All Together' (1999)

We can send you a Delores Smith photo and a T-shirt.

2 Complete the sentences.

Complete these sentences, asking a star for something.

1 I would like ______________________________ .

2 Please send me ______________________________ .

3 I want to ______________________________ please.

4 Could you please ______________________________ .

Writing sentences

3 Work with a partner. Write the sentences (a–c) in the correct place in the dialogue. Then say the dialogue together.

a Can I have your autograph?
b I think you're the best singer in the world.
c When are you going to release a new song?

Melanie dreams that she is talking to her favourite singer, Belinda Peters.

4 Work with a partner. Write five nice things to say to stars you both like.

Example: I've got all your CDs.

Putting sentences together

5 Write two letters from the sentences below. Each letter has two paragraphs.

I watch a lot of English football and I think Liverpool are the best team in the world. I have a question for you: I think you are a really great actress and I want to join your fan club. Please send me an autographed photo of you in a number nine shirt. Who is your favourite actor?

Dear Peter Hurst,

paragraph 1: ______________________________

____

____

paragraph 2: ______________________________

____

____

Dear Delores Smith,

paragraph 1: ______________________________

____

____

paragraph 2: ______________________________

____

____

6 Write a letter to a star (a film star, a sports star or a pop star).

- Say you who are and where you live and how much you like what the star does.
- Write about what the star does (for example you watched the films, or have the CDs).
- Ask the star a question.
- Ask for an autograph or an autographed photo.
- Ask for the address of the fan club so that you can join.

Unit 11 A nice place to live

Writing about your city

Completing sentences

Work with a partner. List buildings in your town or city.

the police station, ______________________________

____

1 Use the essay about a town and the diagram of the town to complete the sentences.

Our town is a nice place to live. At the centre of the town there's the **1** ____________ *Square with the swimming* **2** ____________ *on one side of it. The High Street isn't very interesting. There are a lot of offices in it and a big* **3** ____________ *opposite the offices and a bank and a* **4** ____________ *shop. There's a café I like on the corner of High Street and Main Street. But my favourite places are in Head Road. There are clothes shops there, interesting small* **5** ____________ *shops and a computer* **6** ____________ *where you can get lots of good computer games.*

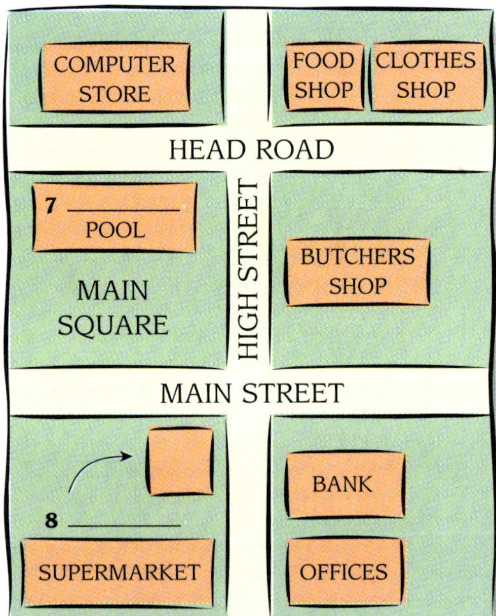

2 Complete the sentences.

Complete these sentences with information about your town or city.

1 The ____________ is near the ____________.

2 The ____________ is opposite the ____________.

3 The ____________ is on one side of the ____________.

Writing sentences

3 Work with a partner. Write the sentences (a–c) in the correct place in the dialogue. Then say the dialogue together.

a I'd like a really good travel shop because I like going to new places.

b I'd like some other excellent shops too, so we can go shopping.

c I'd like a helicopter landing pad because I want to go to school by helicopter.

Laura and Melanie are planning their dream town.

4 Write sentences telling people *why* you want things in your dream city. Use the word *because* in each sentence.

Example: I want a modern library because I like reading

Putting sentences together

5 Write the two sentences again as one sentence using *because* or so.

Examples:

It's our family butcher's shop. I can go there any time I want to.

It's our family butcher's shop so I can go there any time I want to.

I want a big butcher's shop in my dream city. I like lamb for dinner.

I want a big butcher's shop in my dream city because I like lamb for dinner.

1 There's a beautiful park in the centre of the city. People from the offices can go for a walk.

2 There's a bus stop near the cinema. A lot of people want to go home by bus after the film.

3 There is a café near here. We can sit down.

4 There is a café near the shops. A lot of people like to have a cup of coffee after going shopping.

5 I want a helipad near my house. I don't want to walk to school every day.

6 Write a paragraph.

Work with a partner or in a small group. Draw and label a diagram of your dream city. You can start with things from your city that you like and then put on more things. Then write about your dream city.

Write about:

- what there is in the dream city.
- why you like these things.
- why the things are where they are.

Writing Tip

Question: **why?**
Answer: **because**

Unit 12 Dear diary

Writing diary entries

Completing sentences

Write down two things you did last week. Tell your partner about them.

1 ______________________ **2** ______________________

1 Use the story to complete the diary and the diary to complete the story.

Last Monday Robert Simpson went to the Moon. He **1** __________ breakfast with AFP1. AFP1 is a Moon man. He is green and has three arms, three legs, one eye and long, blue hair. He's very clever but he can't ride a **2** __________ very well. On Tuesday Robert taught AFP1 to ride a bicycle. On Wednesday AFP1 and his family (AFP2, 3, 4, 5 and 6) took Robert to see the dark side of the Moon. They went **3** __________ in the sky there. On Thursday they **4** __________ all day. The Moon people eat once a week but they eat a lot. They ate all their tables and chairs and on **5** ____ __________ they made some more.

MONDAY
I went to the Moon. I had **6** __________ with AFP1. We had cornflakes.

TUESDAY
AFP1 is not very good at riding a bicycle. I smiled and said 'Good. Very good.' But he wasn't.

WEDNESDAY
We went swimming. Swimming is very good in the **7** __________, better than in the water.

THURSDAY
We ate from 8 AM Moon time to 6 PM. Tables are delicious on the moon.

FRIDAY
We made some more **8** __________ and chairs because we ate them all yesterday.

2 Complete these sentences.

Last week Robert __________________ but I __________________ .

Last Tuesday Robert __________________ but I __________________ .

When Robert __________________ I __________________ .

Writing sentences

3 Work with a partner. Write the sentences (a–c) in the correct place in the dialogue. Then say the dialogue together.

a It was our first time back there since the move to London.

b All the family enjoyed it.

c I was very busy.

Paul is at Robert's house.

4 Write sentences.

Write seven diary entries for someone else in the class. Write one sentence for each day of the week. Then read your diary entry to your classmate. Were you right about what he or she did?

Putting sentences together

5 Write the two sentences again using *it*.

Examples:

I liked climbing in the mountains.
Climbing in the mountains was fun. (it)

I liked climbing in the mountains. It was fun.

We went to London.
I enjoyed going to London.

We went to London. I enjoyed it.

1 We went swimming.
Going swimming was the best thing we did all week.

2 We played table tennis and football.
I really enjoyed playing table tennis and football.

3 We went shopping a lot.
Going shopping was great.

4 I taught a friend to swim.
Teaching a friend to swim was difficult.

5 I helped my friend with his homework.
I enjoyed helping my friend with his homework very much.

6 Write a diary entry for one week. It can be real or a story.

Write about:

- what you did each day
- how you felt about it all (It was fun. It was terrible.)
- what you ate.

Writing Tip

play – play**ed**
eat – **ate**
do – **did**

Unit 13 It was raining.

Starting stories

Completing sentences

1 Use the story and the picture story to complete the sentences.

It was raining when my brother and I came out of school but when we got to our street the sun was shining again. 'I'm **1** ________________,' said my brother. 'Let's stop at the café for a **2** ______________ of lemonade.'
'What's that?' I said.
'Look! There in the street.'
It was a shirt – a red shirt. Then we saw a **3** ______________ of trousers. Then we saw a pair of **4** ________________.
My brother laughed. Clothes in the street! I laughed too. But then we stopped laughing. We saw the **5** ______________ of a shirt and then one leg of a pair of trousers.
And then we saw the monster.

2 Say sentences to a partner. Then write three of them.

It was The sun was	raining snowing shining	when	I we they	left got to saw	the monster. town on the last train. my house.

1 ____

2 ____

3 ____

Writing sentences

3 Work with a partner. Write the sentences (a–c) in the correct place in the dialogue. Then say the dialogue together.

a 'There was no sun where the monster lived.'
b 'There is a street in our town where nobody ever goes.'
c 'We were walking home from school when we saw the monster.'

Laura and Melanie are writing together at Laura's house.

4 Write some dialogue from your story. You and your friend have just seen the monster for the first time. Write what you both say, then read the dialogues with a partner.

Putting sentences together

5 Write the two sentences again as one sentence with *when* or *where*.

Examples:

The sun was shining. My friend and I saw the monster.

The sun was shining when my friend and I saw the monster.

There is a small café in this street. We live in this street.

There is a small café in the street where we live.

1. I was walking home. I stopped for a drink of lemonade at a café.
2. The café is in a small dark street. Nobody lives in the street.
3. I was feeling unhappy. I saw my friend.
4. I felt bad. I ate all day.
5. This is the big house. The monster lives in the house.

6 Write a paragraph.

Write the first paragraph of a story. Work with a partner or in a small group. Write the start of a story about a monster. Write the opening paragraph – five or six sentences or more. Write some dialogue in your story.

- What was the weather like and what were you doing when you saw the monster?
- What did the monster look like?
- What did you and your friends say? Did the monster speak?
- What happened then?

Writing Tip

When someone speaks, use quotation marks:
'I'm thirsty,' said my brother.

Unit 14 The monster

Continuing and finishing stories

Completing sentences

1 Use the story and the picture story to complete the sentences.

The monster was standing in front of us. There was a red shirt in its hands. It was pointing at the shirt. My brother was afraid. '**1** ______ it!' he shouted. 'Kill the **2** ______!' I was afraid too but I said 'No, wait. The monster wants something.' My brother and I ran back to the café. There was a man there with a mobile phone. I said to him '**3** ______, may I **4** ______ your mobile phone please?' I phoned the police. When the police came they had a red shirt with them. The monster went with the police. Later that evening a policeman came to our house. 'You weren't afraid of the monster,' said the policeman. 'And you were right. The monster was **5** ______ of you. He **6** ______ a man who was like a father to him. This man always wore a red shirt.'

2 Complete the sentences.

Complete these sentences. Use the story to help you.

1 The monster was looking for a man who ______________________ .

2 The police had a red shirt with them when ______________________ .

3 It was later that evening when ______________________ to the boys' house.

Writing sentences

3 Work with a partner. Write the questions (a–c) in the correct place in the dialogue. Then say the dialogue together.

a It's about a man who makes monsters.

b It's a big modern building which has rooms like the science rooms at school.

c They find the monster who has got the boy.

Laura and Melanie are writing together on the train.

4 Write sentences.

Write three sentences of the second paragraph of a story about a monster. The last sentence of the first paragraph is 'And then we saw the monster.'

Putting sentences together

5 Write the sentences again as one sentence using *who* or *which*.

Examples:

The boys found a man.
The man knew about monsters.

The boys found a man who knew about monsters.

The boys found a modern building. The building had rooms like the science rooms at school.

The boys found a modern building which had rooms like the science rooms at school.

1 I knew a boy. The boy told good stories.

2 There was a café near here. The café had three big rooms.

3 We were looking for the monster. The monster had got our friend.

4 My friends found the place. The place was my secret.

5 I wanted to use the mobile phone. The man had the mobile phone in his hand.

6 Write paragraphs of a story.

Work with a partner or in a small group. Write the second and third paragraphs of a story about a monster. The last sentence of the first paragraph is 'And then we saw the monster.'

Writing Tip

who for people
which for things

Pearson Education Limited
Edinburgh Gate
Harlow
Essex CM20 2JE
England

and Associated Companies throughout the world

First published 2000

Second impression 2002

ISBN 0582 41960 3

Set in Avant Garde and Leawood Infant.

Printed in Lebanon by Librairie du Liban.

Prepared for the publishers by Gecko Limited, Granville Way, Bicester, Oxfordshire OX6 OJT.

Acknowledgements

Illustrations by Kathy Baxendale, Chris Brown, Gecko Ltd, Jeffy James, Lorna Kent, Julian Mosedale, Peter Richardson and Andrew Quelch. With special thanks to Lewis Lansford for his contribution as freelance project manager.